21 WAYS TO

Raise Your Vibe

IN 21 DAYS

KERYL PESCE

little pink press™

Cover design by Keryl Pesce

Published by Little Pink Press, Beacon, NY

ISBN-13: 978-1-7372754-7-3

For my tribe.

CONTENTS

It All Begins Here

*It is our absolute promise to you that when you
understand the power of feeling good now, no matter
what, you will hold the key to the achievement of any state
of being, any state of health, any state of wealth,
or any state of anything that you desire.*

-Abraham-Hicks

Hey there! I am so happy you're here. Or, more accurately, I'm there, in your head. Either way, it's great to be together because the truth is I wrote this book for you and me. You see, my highest vibes are when I've shared something I've learned, and as a result, someone like you lives better. And by living better, I mean experiencing less anxiety, fear, and sadness and more inner peace, optimism, and happiness.

I want you to know that I consider our time together an honor. The way I see it, the most precious and valuable places of all are inside your head and heart. So if you choose to invite someone to this sacred ground, you need to know they honor and appreciate that privilege. I do. And I solemnly vow to do my best to leave them both better off.

This book is about the decision to make your happiness a priority and taking deliberate action to elevate your life experience regardless of your current circumstances. Because no matter your situation, there is *always* something you can do to feel, and subsequently, live better. Always. Feeling better *is* living better.

You are about to understand that focusing on how you feel is where it's at. The fact of the matter is, *the better you feel, the better your life becomes*. Your mental, emotional, and physical health improve, your creativity spikes, and new opportunities present themselves to you. You begin to attract ideas, experiences, people, and material manifestations of your desires. Unhealthy thought patterns and feelings loosen their grip. People and circumstances that no longer serve your best interests fade away and drop off, making room for that which aligns with your new energy field, AKA, your vibes.

> *The moment that you find an improved feeling,*
> *conditions and circumstances change*
> *to match your feeling.*
>
> -Abraham-Hicks

Would you like to experience life where frustration is the exception and enjoyment is the rule? Yeah, me too. Let's hang out for a few pages and weeks together and see just how much closer we can get you to that.

The struggle may be real, but it doesn't mean it's right.

I believe those who struggle the most and experience the most stress approach life backward. The thinking is that once their life circumstances become better, then they will feel better. It sounds logical. I get it. I've done it. I have strived, stressed, been pissed off, and frustrated trying *so damn hard* to change people and circumstances around me to feel happier. I was convinced that once I achieved an external change or result, no matter *how much I suffered* to make it happen, it would get me the outcome I wanted. Which ultimately was what? To feel happy. Do you see the irony? "This sucks balls, but damn it, it's gonna make me happy." You can laugh out loud here if you want because I know you can relate. So, yeah, I tried that.

A new route to happy.

Then something shifted. It just didn't make sense to me that the way to be happy later is through being miserable now. Plus, I was tired of everything feeling like such a struggle. So, I tried a new approach. I eased up. I stopped trying so hard (I know, it sounds counterintuitive). I worried and questioned less and went with the flow more. I actively looked for how things played out better when I *allowed* instead of *forced*. And guess what happened? Life became easier, smoother, and a whole lot more enjoyable!

As I settled in, went with the flow, and enjoyed myself more, some pretty amazing stuff played out. I went from feeling like a complete failure, underneath a mountain of credit card debt, and owning investment properties that were upside down (I owed more than they were worth), to being free and clear with recurring monthly income doing what I absolutely love, like writing this book for you.

I hadn't focused on the outcomes, reached them, and then felt better. Instead, I focused on feeling better first, and the outcomes came second.

Focusing on raising your vibe works.

Look at taking on this challenge as deciding to go on a three-week vacation of sorts. Step away from striving and trying so hard. Stop worrying if or how you will perform or how things will work out, and instead make your priority how to feel better right now. This doesn't mean you can stop showing up to school or work, not shower or get dressed, or stop being a mom or caregiver. It means you continue to move through your days with a different energy, one that is less resistant and more open and graceful.

Change doesn't have to be complicated or overwhelming. There is brilliance in simplicity. And, what if rather than carrying the weight of doubt that you are capable of doing what it takes to feel and live better, whether or not you are worthy of the same, or if the circumstances around you will ever improve (they will), you instead set that heavy burden down and choose to take a simpler, lighter approach? Which is to one day at a time, just for that day, choose a Way to feel better.

I'm here to tell you that **small changes have the power to rock your world.**

The low-down on the higher up.

Let's explore a bit how our vibes and energy operate.

Through a field of study known as quantum physics, Nobel-prize-winning physicists have proven that the elemental core of everything in the universe, including you, is energy. This means you literally are a vibrational being in a constant state of energetic communication with everything. This includes plants, animals, other human beings, material objects, and even every cell in your own body. I'll leave the technical aspect there. I'm not here to explain the science. I am here, however, to show you how to use it to your benefit.

If you question the above, I ask you to ponder a few things. Has someone ever walked in a room, and you disliked them before they uttered a word? Or conversely, have you had a good feeling about someone before directly interacting with them? Of course you have. You weren't being judgmental. You were feeling their energy field, their vibe. Have you ever thought of someone, and they simultaneously called or texted? Has a thought or experience ever made every hair on your body stand on end? Have you ever been in a shit mood and not one, but multiple frustrating things happened in succession, including electronic equipment acting wacky? Okay, I think I've made my point.

Bottom line, you are a walking, talking, broadcasting and receiving station. You communicate with and affect *everything* based on your vibrational frequency.

All life is vibration.

-Florence Scovel Shinn

Your vibrational signal is not static or set. It moves on a continuum. At any given moment, you can be anywhere between the lowest levels of energy such as guilt or shame, and the highest of love and joy. You can think of the lower energy frequencies as being heavy and dense and the higher ones as lighter and more open. Your energy levels fluctuate from day to day and even sometimes from moment to moment.

Feeling more enjoyable emotions and aligning the material things, people, and experiences around you to match what you desire is a fluid process. You will have moments of relief and feel better. And you will have moments that feel like you've fallen backward. Don't make a big story about it. Just know it's normal. It's not about a place in life. It's about a *way* of life. So don't give up if you have a crappy day. Welcome to humanity. It happens to all of us. The good news is you now have a new approach and resource at your fingertips to help you raise your vibes back up.

That said, as you repeatedly employ methods such as those that follow, you will elevate your vibrational set point. This means the overall frequency on which you communicate and connect, on average, will become higher and higher.

Will you still at times feel sadness, frustration, anger, etc.? Yes. Not to worry, though. As I will explain later, those feelings are normal, valid, and of value to you. But do I expect you will experience them less frequently and intensely by applying what you learn in the pages ahead? Absolutely!

A bit about the vibrational scale.

As I mentioned above, our energy levels fluctuate and move on a continuum. Let me offer you a further explanation using a visual description. This will help you better identify where you are at any given moment and what vibe-raising options are available to you, depending on your current energetic frequency.

Often, a numerical scale is used to identify where something is within a range, such as a scale of one to ten. Instead, I am going to use color to help guide you.

Flip back to the cover for a moment and take notice of the colors.

The colors at the center are shades of blue. What does feeling blue mean to you? Feeling down and low, right? So the lowest frequencies we experience can be thought of as on the blue end of the color scale. Our lowest vibes are when we feel sad, depressed, unworthy, fearful, hateful, or angry.

As those feelings ease up, you begin to morph into the purples and lavenders. This is the transition away from the intensely low and toward neutral. More neutral vibes are feeling nervous, disappointed, frustrated, bored, or content. Maybe they aren't amazing feelings, but they are an improvement.

As you move further up the scale, the colors turn to magenta and hot pink. These represent positive vibes such as optimism, confidence, hopefulness, and enthusiasm.

And then the gold! Happy, fulfilled, joyful, and loving ... precisely what we all want to experience more of in our lives.

How to get the most out of this book.

Every method I share ahead has worked for me and can for you too, but not every method will be available to you or effective at all times, depending on your current vibe. If you are feeling exceptionally low, and I suggest you go do something fun to raise your vibe, you're going to roll your eyes, close the book, and maybe even toss it in the trash! Because *at that moment*, that specific Way is not within your vibrational reach.

To help you choose an effective Way, I will let you know which ones will be most helpful to you depending on your current vibe/color. A few are universal and will work no matter where you currently find yourself. Some methods are designed to elevate your energy and vibration if you are neutral or already feeling good. Other methods I share involve a lightening of the load, a releasing of heaviness that slows you and your energy down. These are most effective when you feel stuck, stressed, angry, or in a funk. They are designed to get you to a transitional, neutral vibe, so the higher vibe Ways and feelings come within reach.

Some of what I suggest will not be new to you. But a reminder, reinforcement, or new way to employ a practice could certainly be helpful. The fact is, a few of the following methods are fundamental to living a happy and fulfilling life. I would be doing you a disservice if I didn't include them, even simply to serve as a reminder. Some of the Ways that follow will likely be new to you. Have fun giving them a shot!

You may want to read through all of the Ways before you start using them. Then, you'll know all of your options before you begin. Go ahead and dog-ear or bookmark the ones that strike you. Then go back and start with one of those.

Following this section is a quick-start guide which shows you which Ways to use depending on your current state. So, if on a certain day you are feeling blue, you can flip to that page and see which Ways will be helpful.

Near the end of the book are 21 pages for you to list which Way you used that day as well as any notes about what you experienced and felt. I encourage you to take advantage of journaling about your experiences. This could become a great resource in the future to remind yourself of which Ways were most helpful to you.

Do what feels right for you.

As I mentioned, not all Ways will be available to you at all times, but all will be over time. Depending on how you feel in any given moment, only a few might be accessible and effective. Go for what feels within reach. If it feels like too much of a stretch and you aren't sure it will help, skip it. Choose something else.

You may find seven Ways that really resonate with you and do them each three times. Or perhaps just one, 21 times. You may also find that you leverage the vibe-raising power of multiple Ways throughout a given day … whatever works for *you*, whatever feels right and good. Because what feels right and good *is* right and good, so trust that.

Think of this practice as a kind of elixir. The right combination, chosen by you for you, can work miracles. When we give our body what it needs in the form of nutrients, it can and does work miracles. Similarly, when you give your mind and heart what they need, you will manifest, witness, and experience miracles. What you and the person next to you need aren't the same. And even what you need at this moment may not be what you need in the next. Adjust accordingly. Which feels best right now? Do that.

Drop the logic for 21 days. Spend less time in your left side, over-analyzing, critical-thinking brain. We have been told time and time again to use our heads, that we are stronger when we ignore our feelings and do what logic dictates. I've got news for you—your brain is not the wisest part of you. Your feelings are. They know all and are connected to all. Trust them to guide you and make a deliberate choice to give them the love and attention they deserve. Treat your feelings right. Listen to them. Cater to them. Give them what they need to feel appreciated and valued, for they are guiding you every minute of every day, providing you feedback, moment by moment.

The only thing I do strongly suggest is that you commit to doing something each day for at least the next 21 days. After that, you may adopt a few of the Ways as a regular part of how you decide to live your life well beyond the next three weeks.

Better vibes always.

I used to love the phrase "Good vibes only." But the fact is, it's unrealistic to expect good vibes 24/7. This false expectation causes people to think they are failing at life because they don't feel up all the time. And if anyone tells you they do, they're full of shit. Sorry, but that's the truth.

I've come to discover something far better and a whole lot more helpful, and that is "Better vibes always." Meaning there are moments life gets real, and part of being human is sometimes messy. Don't deny it; acknowledge it. When we invalidate the truth of what we feel, we create resistance. Resistance slows and lowers your vibration ... especially if you push against something within you that is a valid aspect of being human. But no matter where you are, reaching for a better vibe is *always* possible. And sometimes, that better vibe is simply a little bit of relief. Sometimes happiness isn't instantly within reach in a certain moment, but a little less hopelessness or sadness is. So you may not immediately jump from desperately low to bursting with joy, but you can move closer. And closer is good. *Really* good. Because even just a little at a time, anyone can get there.

It is not a difficult thing to change the pattern
of your vibration, especially when you understand
that you can do it a little bit at a time.

-Jerry and Esther Hicks

Flap your wings.

I want you to spend more time in the bright pink and gold zones of life. I want this for your benefit and enjoyment and for the countless others who will be affected by your vibes and energy field. Good vibes are *extremely* contagious. According to one of my favorite people and author of *Get Out of the Red Zone*, Dr. Elizabeth Lombardo, "...when you are happier, not only are the people around you happier, but so are the people around them. There are two degrees of separation (at least) when it comes to positive energy." So the better you feel, the better others feel, and so on and so on. Deliberately raising your vibes sends energetic ripples that will positively affect families, neighborhoods, and the world as a whole. I'd say it's high time *that's* the kind of contagion we give our energy and attention to. Wouldn't you agree?

I am a believer of the butterfly effect.
A small positive vibration can change the entire cosmos.

-Amit Ray

Best of all, none of what I suggest requires anything or anyone around you to change. That means the power to raise your vibe rests entirely with you. You got this, and I got you. And although nothing need change around you for you to start raising your vibe, just watch what actually *does* change in the form of people, opportunities, and synchronicities.

Ready? Let's do this!

Quick Start Guide

Ways within reach depending on your current vibe/color:

Blue

WAYS # 2, 3, 4, 5, 6, 7, 8, 10, 13, 14, 15, 16, 17

Lavender/Purple

WAYS # 1, 2, 3, 4, 5, 6, 7, 8, 9, 10, 11, 12, 13, 14, 15, 16, 17, 18, 20, 21

Magenta

WAYS # 1, 2, 4, 5, 6, 8, 9, 10, 11, 12, 13, 14, 15, 16, 17, 18, 19, 20, 21

Pink

WAYS # 1, 2, 4, 5, 6, 8, 9, 11, 12, 13, 14, 15, 16, 17, 18, 19, 20, 21

Gold

WAYS # 1, 2, 4, 5, 6, 8, 9, 11, 12, 13, 14, 15, 16, 17, 18, 19, 20, 21

IT'S TIME TO RISE

WAY #1

Know What You Really Want

(LAVENDER TO GOLD)

*The foundation of a good relationship with
intentions and goals is keeping in mind that the
primary aim of setting and working toward
them is to feel the way you want to feel.*

-Danielle LaPorte

Do you ever doubt your ability to achieve your goals because working toward them feels like such a struggle? Have you ever achieved what you set out to, but the satisfaction and happiness you expected fell short or were short-lived? It's not you. It's how you've been taught to set goals.

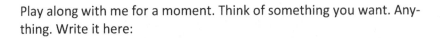

Play along with me for a moment. Think of something you want. Anything. Write it here:

When you achieve or acquire this, how do you expect to feel? Write that here:

Guess what, my friend? Your first answer is not what you really want. Your second answer is.

What you *really* want is the feeling you expect to experience, not the car, job, partner, dress size; I could go on. My point is you are after an internal state. We all are.

> *You're not chasing the goal itself—*
> *you're chasing the feelings that you hope*
> *attaining those goals will give you.*

> -Danielle LaPorte

This is not to say you shouldn't want the first goal. I want you to have everything your precious heart desires. However, I want you to work toward that outer accomplishment you desire with the awareness that your ultimate goal is an internal state of being ... a feeling. Otherwise, you risk losing your way or getting stuck in a major rut. You may become miserable and stressed now, believing it will result in your happiness later. You may very well (and many of us *do*) end up on a journey that creates the exact opposite feeling NOW that you believe you are on your way to experience in the future. Can you say holding pattern?

Here's how this often goes. We set out to accomplish something, whatever that may be ... buy a new car, lose 20 pounds, make more money, all valid goals. And the reason we set these goals is the expectation of how we will feel once achieved ... some level of personal goodness; happy, proud, good enough, etc. Then we turn into dumb asses. Our ultimate goal is to feel good, right? Except we set out on the journey to get there with worry, fear, stress, a must-accomplish-or-I'm-a-loser-failure attitude, losing sleep, acting like an asshole to whoever is in earshot because "I HAVE TO MAKE THIS HAPPEN so I can feel good!" Can you at least laugh at the insanity of it?

Is there a time for pushing yourself to the finish line and putting in extra work? Of course. There are moments in life that call for this. But if we completely lose sight that the very reason we set out on the journey is to feel good, and we are effing miserable en route, well, we've missed the goal right out of the gate. The target is happiness or any positive variation of that feeling, and often we end up shooting ourselves in the foot, limping through life. Mind your target.

Will we all encounter stumbles, frustrations, roadblocks, or worse? You can count on it. When the energy behind that delay or frustration is fear and anger because we HAVE to make this happen *in order to* be happy and feel proud or confident, ooh, baby, have we got a recipe for stress and anxiety!

If, however, we have taken the time to get clear on the internal states we desire *first* and then map out some external goals we'd like to achieve, well, you've got an entirely different ride. This allows you, moment by moment, to make some pretty wise and empowered choices on your journey. This will enable you to adjust course or sometimes even abandon course from a place of clarity because you are finally clear on what really matters to you.

By the way, quitting is not necessarily a weak choice. Sometimes, quitting is a brilliant and empowered choice. If you are in touch with your ultimate goal and are aware and present enough, it can be the smartest thing you ever do. If something is sucking the soul right out of you, and you blindly stick with it, does that make you smart and successful? Hard pass for me.

When you maintain awareness of the inner state you desire, and an un-expected roadblock comes up, your fear and self-doubt don't come raging up. You don't hit the panic button. Instead, you pause, reconnect to what is most important, and ask your wise self, "OK, what next? What's the next best step?" You stay connected to your desired internal state as you move toward your external goal. So the outcome can be fantastic and something to celebrate, and the journey to get there can be as well.

It bears repeating. You are a vibrational being in a vibrational universe. You communicate with, respond to, and influence *everything* energetically. As you learn to focus on your internal state and practice feeling good now, you elevate your ability to manifest and achieve your external desires.

Without exception, my most enjoyable achievements occurred when I had excited anticipation about the process and the outcome. I overwhelmingly felt good in the process of bringing my goals to fruition. I felt good before I got "there." I felt good on the way "there." I'm not saying there wasn't effort, discomfort, or frustration along the way, or that there weren't moments I wanted to throat-punch someone, including myself if it were possible. There were. There always will be. But my dominant vibration was excitement, backed by an understanding of what I desired most. Oh, what a magical combination that is!

This Way is designed to help you gain clarity on what you truly desire—the internal state. Getting in touch with and knowing this is what you are really after makes all of your other goal-setting more powerful, effective, and most important, in alignment with your inner truth and your most powerful energetic frequencies.

This exercise is inspired by one of the most incredible books I've ever read, and that is "The Desire Map" by Danielle LaPorte. I love this book so much. It helped me see with complete clarity how traditional goal setting is backward and the real reason my past successes came to fruition.

This is a much-abbreviated version, but it will get you started. If this strikes a good vibe with you, by all means, get her book, read it cover to cover, and do the exercises she suggests. Major power play. Major vibe raiser.

Think back on a time or times when you felt really good. This is where you return to and remember the internal state you enjoy and value the most. Get in touch with these feelings again, remember how they felt, and bring them forward to you in the present moment. Describe what you did or what was going on. Most importantly, write down how you felt:

Next, answer this: What do I want to feel more of in my life? (Some of these may be the same as above.)

To dive slightly deeper into this exercise, look up some of the words in an online dictionary or thesaurus. Then, add any words that feel good to you and write them here:

Now go back and review and circle 3-5 words or phrases from above that resonate most with you and write them here:

As you go about your day, stay in touch with these words and keep asking yourself, "What can I do that will bring more of these feelings to my experience today? What thoughts or perspectives can I choose? What can I let go of and/or walk away from?" If you want to take this further, take a little more time and think about some actions and longer-term goals that might bring more of these feelings into your life experience. Write them down here:

Knowing that your primary goal is the feeling you wish to experience and staying in touch with that will seriously amp up your ability to achieve your external goals. You are clear. You KNOW what you want. And from that knowing, that chosen priority, you move with grace and power toward the external accomplishment. Not the other way around.

Today, allow yourself to move through your day with these core desired feelings in mind.

WAY #2

Let Someone Know the Positive Impact They've Had on You

(BLUE TO GOLD)

By seeing the best in other people,
you will put yourself in a phenomenal vibration.

-Bob Proctor

One of my very good friends and co-host on Happy Hour is Jonna Spilbor. She is an attorney who owns a successful law practice and has had hundreds of appearances on national television weighing in on legal issues. She is super intelligent, gorgeous, and funny. If you told her I said this about her, she wouldn't be surprised, and that's not because she's conceited. It's because I am not shy about telling her the good I see in her. When I reinforce the positive I see in her, *I* feel good. It raises both her vibe and mine.

Appreciation is a wonderful thing.
It makes what is excellent in others belong to us as well.

-Voltaire

I have another close friend, Dave, who was my mentor and taught me how to successfully invest in real estate. Because of his generosity of time and knowledge, I am self-employed and have the privilege of working from home and on projects such as writing this book that are immensely fulfilling. My life is infinitely better because of him being in it. He taught me how to become financially free, so I decide what I want to do and when. This is priceless to me. Should you ever meet or speak to him and tell him you read this, he too, would not be surprised. I have told him countless times how much he has changed my life and how grateful I am.

I make it a regular practice to let the people I appreciate know how I feel. I know it makes them feel good. And you know what? It makes me feel even better. It is like an act of kindness wrapped in a package of gratitude. This Way of raising your vibe gives you a double boost.

I've also been on the receiving end. Jonna and I probably share thousands of texts in a year. I'm not exaggerating. Not a week goes by, between planning shows and guests, venting, or sharing humorous stories that we aren't communicating. There is one text she sent me a few years back that I will remember as long as I live. Out of the blue, I received a text from her that said, "Having you as a friend makes me feel like I've done something right in this life." Can you imagine how you would feel if someone said this to you, particularly someone you care about and respect very much? She gave me a gift that day which I will treasure always.

We all have people in our lives, whether they are friends, relatives, former teachers or bosses, who have impacted us in a positive way. Some, who perhaps even completely altered the course of our lives for the better. They deserve to know the difference they've made.

There is more hunger for love and appreciation in this world than for bread.

- Mother Teresa

Who has made your life better and how? Tell them today. Let them know you appreciate the impact they've had on your life.

WAY #3

Allow Space for the Feels

(BLUE TO LAVENDER)

Your emotions make you human.
Even the unpleasant ones have a purpose.
Don't lock them away. If you ignore them,
they just get louder and angrier.

-Sabaa Tahir

One of the unfortunate fallouts from the positive-thinking movement is that many of us fear any thought or feeling we experience that isn't "positive". We falsely believe being positive means feeling up and happy all of the time, and if a negative thought or emotion shows up (and it will), something must be wrong with us. So what do we do? We judge and push against the negative thoughts and feelings, creating internal resistance and conflict. Us against us. Then what happens? Say "Hello" to anxiety, depression, exhaustion, and a sense of failing at being us and all we are capable of. Without realizing what we are doing, we amplify and give an immense amount of power to the very thing we want less of. If you read my book, *Hello Beautiful*, I share the depths I took this to and how it affected me.

I'm not a medical professional, but my personal experience has shown me that if you deal with bouts of depression or anxiety, the possibility exists that there is nothing at all wrong with you that needs fixing. The only issue is a false belief causing you to wage a war against yourself where a battle need not take place in the first place.

> *It's a curious truth that when you gently pay attention*
> *to negative emotions, they tend to dissipate—*
> *but positive ones expand.*

-Oliver Burkeman

I have painfully learned firsthand that our "negative" emotions don't go away when we try to avoid or ignore them. In fact, the more energy we give to suppressing them, the more they fester, amplify, and ultimately show up in our lives, often as physical ailments. Here's the real deal: all human emotions are normal. All are necessary. All have the capacity to serve us. We are not helping ourselves by brushing them under the rug and pretending they aren't there. They are. And that's okay.

A much more productive and healthier approach is to allow space for them without resistance and then mine for and process the wisdom they hold. This is highly effective to alleviate that which holds you at a lower frequency thereby allowing you to elevate your vibe. However, you will need the courage and willingness to go "down" to come back up.

When we effectively process our emotions and experiences, it is like untying the knot that attaches a heavy weight to our ankle. We release its grip and float up. It's *incredibly* liberating.

So today, be open to the possibility that all emotions are normal and are not meant to be ignored, avoided, or judged. If a bit of anxiety, sadness, self-doubt, or anger creep in, simply notice it. Allow it to be there. Rather than negatively judging these feelings (which intensifies and prolongs them), simply be aware of them and do one of two things. One, silently tell yourself, "This too shall pass," because it will. Emotions are fluid. Or two, if you have the time and are in a position to do so, become curious about it. Don't kick it out of your mental house. Yes, it is an uninvited guest, but be gracious. Sit down with it. Ask the emotion how it wants to help you and what positive action you can take. You will gain wisdom, and the negative feeling will release itself from you. At the very least, it will lessen, and your vibes will move higher.

This Way may seem counterintuitive, but it is a powerful method to release what may be holding you at a lower vibrational frequency.

WAY #4

(pronounced flõ·er)

(BLUE TO GOLD)

Light and flow is what shifts the world's vibration,
not the stagnation and resistance
that comes with opposition.

-Alaric Hutchinson

We humans are notorious for our desire for control and certainty. We plan out our days, incessantly making mental lists of what needs to happen and get done in what order. We believe we will be happy, content, or at peace if all goes according to plan. And how often does it really? The desire to control outcomes is a huge stressor. It is actually rooted in fear.

Move, but don't move the way fear makes you move.

-Rumi

We are afraid if we don't constantly think, evaluate, and calculate, things won't work out for the best. We believe that planning and worrying best ensure the outcomes we desire. But do they? Is our controlling nature trying to *control* Nature? And is that a futile effort? Are we communicating to the cosmos that we do not trust the incredible brilliance and power that surrounds and permeates us by doing so? And does our lack of trust and faith actually attract more circumstances that align with the energetic frequency of our worry? Hmmm, how can I put this? Hell yeah!

What the universe will manifest when you are
in alignment with it is a lot more interesting than
what you try to manifest.

-Adyahsanti

Through much stress and heartache, I have learned to loosen the grip and go with the flow if things don't pan out exactly as I envisioned. Rather than hit the panic button, I tap the faith button. I may initially feel frustrated. I mean, I am human, after all. But I quickly bring myself to a place of faithful curiosity. "OK, this kind of sucks. It wasn't how I expected things to go, but what if something better plays out?"

What if something better plays out? Well, what if?

Have you ever gone through something that sucked at the time, and in retrospect, it turned out to be a really good thing? Me too. The truth is, some pretty amazing things happened as a result of my prayers *not* being answered.

Faith is like a muscle that becomes stronger the more you use it. It takes practice, but wow, can this be a life-changing, vibe-raising practice! There have been so many times that I enjoyed outcomes better than I ever could have imagined or stressed to achieve by letting go and allowing things to unfold. There is magic all around us. It wants to do its thing. It wants to bring you joy, love, happiness, and fulfillment. But sometimes, when we have a tight grip on exactly how things should play out, we choke it off.

I get that this might seem foreign to you, as you have likely had it drilled in your head to set specific, measurable goals and work your ass off until achieved. There is a time for that, but there are far more opportunities in your life to know the bigger picture of what you want to achieve (ahem, the feeling, as we have already discussed), working and doing your part, and being open and flexible as you do.

> *...when you stop trying to make things happen,*
> *anything can.*
>
> -Tosha Silver

So today, I invite you to take on this approach. Choose to be open and flexible. With a sense of curiosity, allow your day to unfold, rather than stressing and striving to control outcomes. Go with the flow. Tap into a bit of trust that all will work out. Stay present and aware and on the lookout for things to unfold naturally ... maybe even magically.

WAY #5

Be Billy for a Day

(BLUE TO GOLD)

Change your words to change the vibration.

-Michael Losier

I named this Way after my awesome neighbor, who unknowingly taught me a thing or two about the power of our words. I'll explain more shortly. First, a little background.

The words we choose are priceless tools we use to communicate. We can give direction and advice, teach, express love and admiration, and define and describe experiences and observations through speaking or writing. This is not news to you. What may be news, however, is that the words we choose are not only used to *describe* our experiences.

They are capable of influencing and shaping them. Our words are acts of creation. In fact, Abracadabra in Hebrew translates to "I will create as I speak."

Your word is your wand, filled with magic and power.

-Florence Scovel Shinn

You've heard that thoughts become things and have the power to shape our worlds. Words carry even more power, as they become the physical expression of our thoughts. Think of words as Thoughts 2.0. The words we choose affect how we feel, and how we feel affects how we energetically show up and influence the world around us.

Let's play a little with some word choices to illustrate my point. Take notice of the difference in how they feel.

Say this aloud: "This is a problem."

Now, try this: "This is a challenge."

Similarly, "The problem is...."

Now, "The challenge is...."

One implies a roadblock. The other suggests something to figure out. One tells your subconscious and the universe, "This sucks." The other says, "Hmmm, I need to figure this out."

Try it again and notice where your thoughts go after saying each. Next time you catch yourself about to use the word "problem," replace it with "challenge" and notice where that takes you.

Here's another subtle yet powerful shift in words.

When we feel a "negative" emotion, we are accustomed to saying "I am sad," or "I am angry." And while that may be an accurate description of what you feel in that moment, the emotion doesn't define you.

What's the alternative? "I *feel* sad," or "I *feel* angry."

Feelings are something you have;
not something you are.

-Shannon L. Alder

The change in word choice is subtle, but massively different. One causes you to identify with the emotion. The other recognizes it is a feeling that comes and goes. The latter is the truth. You are not the emotion. You are you, temporarily experiencing a feeling. Saying "I feel..." vs. "I am..." allows you to move through the negative emotion and on to a better-feeling one.

Another word practice that can raise your vibe comes into play when you experience something uncomfortable or upsetting and discuss it with someone else. Venting is a helpful release, especially if done with the right people. The key to making venting most beneficial is to not end with the vent. Instead, close with something productive or positive.

For example, a co-worker pissed you off, and you vent to another co-worker. "Lisa left her work unfinished again. She is so freaking lazy." This may be true, but don't let it end there. Don't end down. End up. "And I look forward to the day she starts pulling her weight."

It's okay to go down, so long as you also turn back up. Otherwise, your words will reinforce the negative situation. Keep the door open to improvement. If this is hard for you when you are frustrated, start by making a game of it. Even if you say it jokingly, you just might see some of your "end ups" coming true.

Do you have an ongoing to-do list? Instead of calling it your "to-do list", try referring to it as your "get to-do list". Seriously, if you lost everything tomorrow, what about today would you be grateful for? The fact is, many of the things we do truly are a privilege. COVID 19 brought this front and center when we suddenly lost our ability to hug friends, go out to dinner, and even see family. Pause for a moment and think about how many people would consider it a privilege to "get" to stop and pick up the dry cleaning, rake the yard, or wash the dishes.

We craft our world by what we say.

-Tosha Silver

When I first left my ex after discovering his affair, and the intense emotions settled down, I used my words to shape the reality I now enjoy. I remember holding my hands together, palms up, and saying to people, "My whole world is in my hands now. I get to choose what I want it to look like." I spoke more of what I wanted to see and experience in my life than what I didn't. My life unfolded according to the words I chose.

One of the most destructive ways we use our words is how we choose to talk to ourselves. Drop, spill, or break something? "A-hole! You can't even do a simple thing right!" I've done this more times than I can count. Keeping it real. Then I catch myself and say, "I can do better." Or, simply, "Oops."

Also, with your self-talk, keep an eye out for the word "should." I am not a fan of should-ing on ourselves. It implies shame. Almost any time we use the word "should" with ourselves, or even with others for that matter, we can choose to replace it with "could."

Check it out: "I should work out." Ugh.

Now, "I could work out."

Can you feel the difference? One implies we better do it; the other suggests we can do it. Completely different vibes.

And if your self-talk involves negative labels such as "I'm a failure," "I'm a loser," or "I'm not good enough," you can make one small shift that immediately lessens the intensity of what you feel. Instead, say, "I'm having the thought that I'm a failure," "I'm having the thought that I'm a loser," or "I'm having the thought that I'm not good enough." This is a *major* power play. You no longer identify as the label and recognize it's only a current thought you hold. A thought, by the way, that you have chosen. Choose better.

So here's where the name came from for this Way. My neighbor Billy is an awesome guy. Just seeing him makes me smile. He is always in a good mood, easy-going, and gives off amazing vibes. No matter what we discuss, he closes the conversation or subject matter with, "It's all good." Every time. Without fail. I get a kick out of having friends or family over, and I tell them about Billy and what he does. Then I introduce them to him, and guess what? He says it. "It's all good."

What a great message to communicate to yourself, others, and the universe. If you discuss something positive, it's like an exclamation point, reinforcing the goodness. If it's neutral, you end higher, and if it's negative, you instill faith and trust that all will work out.

I love talking with Billy, knowing that no matter what we discuss, the last thing he will say to me is, "It's all good." And I always reply with, "It *is* all good, Billy," and I smile and walk away with higher vibes than before I spoke to him.

> *The word is the most powerful tool you have as a human;*
> *it is the tool of magic.*
>
> -Don Miguel Ruiz

He's creating magic with his choice of words. He reassures himself all is well and simultaneously raises the vibes of those he speaks to. Imagine this becoming a habit and automatic for you. Imagine those who talk to *you* walking away smiling and a bit higher up the vibrational scale because of a simple yet powerful choice of words on your part. Be Billy for a day. And maybe tomorrow and the next and the next.

Today, choose your words mindfully to raise your vibes and the vibes of those around you.

WAY #6

Connect with Nature

(BLUE TO GOLD)

In every walk with nature,
one receives far more than he seeks.

-John Muir

It is widely understood that connecting with nature is good for us. Organizations such as the American Heart Association, The National Institutes of Health, and the American Psychological Association support that connecting with nature is good for our health. It has been shown to reduce blood pressure, heart rate, muscle tension, and anxiety. It can boost our mood, creativity, and happiness. I can't help but wonder if one of the reasons mental-health issues such as anxiety, ADHD, and depression are so much higher today in adults and children than a few decades ago is due to the increased use of technology and decreased time spent outside.

When I was a kid, I spent a lot of time outdoors. I'd play games like hide and seek and kick the can with the neighborhood kids. I'd climb trees, lay on the ground looking up at the sky to watch for shooting stars, and build mini-cities in the dirt. Some of my fondest childhood memories are camping in tents with my family, sitting around a fire, and eating and sleeping outdoors. While some may still experience their childhood like this today, it seems to be more the exception.

In many ways we are so wonderfully connected with each other and to information through technology. Personally, I can't imagine not having the ability to have instant communication with friends and family via texting. I am grateful for it. Yet, at the same time, our connection to technology also creates a disconnection with nature.

Nature is brilliant beyond comprehension and powerful beyond measure. Brilliant and powerful are two things I'm interested in aligning with.

Have you ever gone on a hike and felt calmed, walked through a park in the spring and felt optimistic, or been awestruck by a sunset or rainbow? Nature is the source of all life, and when we connect with and appreciate her, we physically feel more alive. She wants to infuse you with more life and vitality. So why not make a conscious effort to open that window and let her?

> *Look deep into nature,*
> *and then you will understand everything better.*
>
> -Albert Einstein

I realize not all of us can take hour-long walks in the woods every day, but options are always available. Here are several ways you can quite literally recharge yourself and reconnect with nature:

-Go for a walk outside. If you are in an urban setting surrounded by buildings and sidewalks, try sitting outside and looking at the sky. No matter where you live, you can do this.

-Stand barefoot on the earth. Known as earthing, research shows that doing so results in increased antioxidants, reduced inflammation, and improved sleep. There is even evidence of an energy exchange between humans and the earth's surface. There is a known vast supply of electrons on the surface of the earth. We benefit from the energetic exchange when we walk or stand barefoot on the ground.

-Watch videos or documentaries about nature and Planet Earth.

-Plant a vegetable or flower garden and become actively involved in supporting nature to create and foster life.

-Plant vegetable or flower seeds indoors and know that your involvement literally created life.

-Purchase a house plant and focus daily on helping it thrive.

-Go to a park.

-Sit near a stream, river, lake, or ocean.

There are so many options for you to choose from. Do something that feels right for you. Make a conscious and deliberate effort to connect with the very brilliance that gives and supports life and take notice of how that feels.

WAY #7

(BLUE TO LAVENDER)

The best advice I can give to anyone
going through a rough patch is to never
be afraid to ask for help.

-Demi Lovato

I have a few girlfriends with whom I communicate at least a few times a week via group text. Overwhelmingly, we share images, insight, or updates that spread positive vibes. It is always a mood-booster when I see a text pop up from one of these girls. I can't even tell you how much fun stuff we have shared with each other and the smiles and outright laughter I've experienced as a result.

While these girls and the rest of my inner circle are pretty high vibers, we are not fair-weather friends. We don't run for the hills when another has a bad day or goes through something significant. We stick around. We check-in, support each other, and sometimes most important of all, validate each other's feelings. There are times to do what you can to raise someone's vibe, and there are times to meet them where they are and give them space and permission to feel however they feel.

So while we are quick to lift each other, we are also not shy to share in our struggles, knowing we will be understood and supported.

I recently received a text from a good friend simply asking if I could talk, that she could use some positive vibes. I replied, "Now is good," and dropped what I was doing to speak with her. I consider it a privilege that my friends feel safe to open up to me, and they trust me to be heard and expect they will feel better as a result. She did.

*The strong individual is the one who asks for
help when he needs it.*

-Rona Barrett

The fact is, we should never feel ashamed for needing and asking for help from others. It's not being weak. It's being human and operating within a framework that began thousands of years ago. There was a time in human evolution when we needed to be part of a tribe for our physical survival. Count on others for support or die, basically. One person alone was not likely to survive long if they needed to take full responsibility to find shelter, kill for food, and fight off saber-toothed tigers. Unless, of course, you're Katniss Everdeen, contemporary, fictional badass.

So while our immediate and basic survival needs are no longer dependent on being part of a tribe, I think our emotional survival needs are. I don't think we were ever designed for or intended to go it alone, especially if we are struggling, whether it be with a more serious condition such as clinical depression or simply feeling low, unsure, or doubting our worth.

Ask for help. Receiving is an act of generosity.

-Cheryl Richardson

We all have people in our lives who care about us. All you need is one. So if today is a day you are feeling down, reach out to one of them. Open up. Allow a little vulnerability to enter. Ask for support. Ask for a boost.

WAY #8

Be a Good Human

(BLUE TO GOLD)

*Compassion has certain vibration-
vibration that resonates with the cosmos.*

-Amit Ray

When I was a little girl, our family did not have much money. My dad was often gone, as he worked two jobs to take care of my mom, my two sisters, and me. Making ends meet was definitely a challenge. I remember more than once, my mother at the kitchen table with bills in front of her, crying. We used to get free lunches at school, which, as a kid, I thought was cool. I didn't realize what that meant for where my parents stood financially.

One evening, near Christmas, there was a knock at the door. My mom answered it, and there stood people holding boxes of food for us. They had done a food drive at the school, and we were one of the families who benefited.

I may not recall what I had for dinner last night or the night before, but I remember this night very clearly, even though it was decades ago. It is my earliest memory of the capacity of humans to be generous and kind without the expectation of anything in return. Our family was better off because people chose to help us. They neither judged us nor cared if we knew who they were. They chose to help one of their own kind ... other humans.

We hear an awful lot today about people identified by a label – white, black, LGBTQ, poor, wealthy, liberal, conservative, and on and on and on. While I fully understand the needs and desires of those within a particular category may differ from another, I feel we focus on our differences too much. As a result, we create divisiveness and lose sight of that which unites and connects us ... our humanity.

If you look up the definition of humanity in Merriam-Webster, you will find the following: "compassionate, sympathetic, or generous behavior or disposition, the quality or state of being human," with the example of "joined together by their common humanity."

The dictionary literally defines us by what we share in common: being compassionate and generous. What a beautiful collective label we all have.

When we choose to be kind to another person, without any judgments or expectations, we show up as our best selves, demonstrating and experiencing what it means to be human. We feel good about ourselves, and when that happens, I am convinced that we are in touch with the very truth of who we are.

When you carry out acts of kindness,
you get a wonderful feeling inside. It is as though
something inside your body responds and says,
yes, this is how I ought to feel.

-Harold Kushner

If you want the fastest route to raising your vibe no matter where you are on the vibrational scale, offer up a kind and thoughtful gesture toward another person. The results are instantaneous.

Be a good human today. Look for an opportunity to do an act of kindness for someone you know, someone you love, or maybe even someone you've never met. This could be one of the Ways you choose to make a regular part of your daily routine. It is a sure-fire Way to instantly lift your vibe at the moment and steadily raise your vibrational set point over time.

This is my favorite Way to raise vibes. No matter where you currently are on the vibrational scale, it works. Any time. Any day. No matter what.

> *I've been searching for ways to heal myself,*
> *and I've found that kindness is the best way.*
>
> -Lady Gaga

WAY #9

Bring Back that High-Vibing Feeling

(LAVENDER TO GOLD)

Find a place where there's joy,
and the joy will burn out the pain.

-Joseph Campbell

We've discussed how our thoughts and feelings have energetic frequencies that communicate with and affect all things around and within us. There's something else you ought to know. They love a good party.

When you have a negative thought, such as not being worthy or good enough, an invitation goes out for other similar thoughts to join in. In fact, our memories are stored with other memories that match the feeling associated with them, good or bad. In other words, our bodies file our memories in similar-feeling folders.

Have you ever made a mistake, felt like crap about it, and then went looking for all the other reasons besides this one instance that you are a loser and your life sucks? Yeah, me too. We opened a shit-feeling file drawer.

You've heard the expression "train of thought." This is what it refers to. And sometimes, it's a freight train that has gained momentum because so many like thoughts have hopped on.

It's terrific when it's a fun party, such as when something exciting or really great has happened, or you feel empowered and confident, and all your good-feeling thoughts hop on board. We all love those times. However, the reality is that life can be challenging. Conditions aren't always ideal. Unfortunately, the party happening inside our heads is not always a good one. But we go hang out there anyway out of habit. Think about it. If someone texted you and said, "Hey, come on over later. A bunch of mean jerks, some angry dudes, and a few people who feel sorry for themselves are going to hang out for a while," would you have any interest in going? Me neither. Yet, we do this all the time in our heads.

People deal too much with the negative,
with what is wrong. Why not try and see positive things,
to just touch those things and make them bloom?

-Thich Nhat Hanh

It's not your fault, really. It's your biology. We have neural pathways in our brains, and our thoughts like to follow the most familiar and worn route. This is why most people who are Negative Nellies tend to stay that way most of their lives. But even if you consider yourself a negative person, you have the capacity to change that because we all have what is known as neural plasticity, meaning we are capable of creating new neural pathways in our brains. Yes, you can rewire your brain, in a very literal sense. As you repeatedly decide to forge new paths, the old ones shrink up, and the new ones become the easy ones to take.

It takes but one positive thought
when given a chance to survive and thrive
to overpower an entire army of negative thoughts.

-Robert H. Schuller

One of the best ways to rewire your thought patterns and send your thoughts down a positive path is to recall past experiences that bring forth good feelings. The key is to do this with gratitude and appreciation for the experience. Bring forth both the memory *and* the good feeling that goes with it.

Pause here and recall some great memories, times of joy, fun, laughter, and/or feeling proud of yourself. When did you laugh so hard you could hardly breathe? When did you accomplish something you set out to do? When did you feel appreciated? Loved? Write down the experience and what you felt here:

This process will immediately raise your vibe. Then when your vibe needs a boost in the future, come back here and bring your thoughts to these memories, and let the good-feeling party start. And by all means, keep a running list.

If you are a visual person, you could have a great time creating a "win wall". This is sort of like a dream board, but instead, you post words or pictures of what you already love and appreciate about yourself, your life, and things you possess or have experienced.

Invite your good thoughts and feelings to hang out with you today.

This Way will raise your vibe today and is also a great Way to make part of your daily routine.

WAY #10

(BLUE TO MAGENTA)

Forgive others not because they deserve forgiveness,
but because you deserve peace.

-Jonathan Lockwood Huie

As I explained earlier, some Ways are designed to lighten the load and help you ease up on what's holding you down. This is one of them. The release and lightness possible by doing this can have a massive positive impact on your vibration and energy. As you experience relief from the heaviness, you expand your reach of accessible Ways.

Call me Captain Obvious, but people will let you down, or worse, screw you over. Unfortunately, it often ends up being people close to us. There's nothing like trusting and allowing someone in your life and heart, and they do something that completely obliterates both. Perhaps you can relate.

In my first book, *Happy Bitch*, I share how the discovery of my ex's affair devastated me at the time. It was a deeply low point in my life. Fear, pain, and a bottle of antacids were my constant companions. Then the day came when I was ready to move away from the hurt and anger and toward what I wanted, which was to be happy again.

I knew that deliberately hurting him back would not bring me closer to what I wanted. Within just a few weeks of the discovery, I told my ex I didn't want to fight, that there was enough hurt and pain, and I didn't want to cause more. He agreed. We didn't fight. True story.

Now, could you make the case he deserved to be hurt after what he did? Sure. Most would. Most people, after being hurt, engage in a downward spiral of tit for tat, feeling self-righteous in doing so. I understand. I really do. But here's the thing. Although people will do wrong by you, *you* can always do right by you. Putting your energy into hurting someone back is not doing right by you. When you respond with anger and resentment intending to cause another discomfort or pain, you hurt yourself. You waste your precious energy. You drop your vibrational signal like a rock.

> *How people treat you is their karma;*
> *how you react is yours.*
>
> -Wayne W. Dyer

So maybe some people decide not to deliberately hurt back, which is great, but they choose to hold a grudge, which is not so great. The typical view here is that we are strong by staying angry and not forgiving. As a result, former lovers become haters, and siblings or former friends live out decades, never speaking again, believing they are stronger due to their resolve. It may be common, but it's misguided.

I get the guarded heart. When we suffer pain, we want to keep it from ever happening again, so we throw up a wall of resentment, expecting it to protect us. But it's not just one wall. It's four walls, and it becomes a mental and emotional prison.

> *As I walked out the door toward the gate*
> *that would lead to my freedom, I knew if I didn't*
> *leave my bitterness and hatred behind,*
> *I'd still be in prison.*

-Nelson Mandela

When someone hurts you, and you *choose* resentment (yes, it's a *chosen* response), you give power away over your happiness and joy. You hand it right the eff over. "Here you go, a-hole, I am your miserable puppet. Go ahead and pull my strings for the rest of my life." Am I right, or am I right? And who, my friend, are you giving that power to? *Someone who doesn't deserve it*. There is only one person in this world who deserves that kind of power, and that person is you.

This book is all about consciously making choices that free you from emotional burdens, elevate your energy and vibration, and bring you more happiness and joy. Remaining angry is remaining stuck in the mud. It's impossible to jump for joy from there.

Cut the strings. You are nobody's puppet.

When you decide to forgive, it is one of the most loving and powerful actions you can take – for *you*. You don't have to work to forget what happened in the past or wish to change it. Your work is in the right now to no longer allow it to hold you back and hold you down. Make no mistake, forgiveness is a sign of strength. It is a major power move. You make your happiness and joy more important than hanging on to resentment. Love yourself more than you hate the other. They don't even need to know you forgave them. It doesn't have anything to do with them at all. It's all about you.

If you feel this Way is what you need, get yourself someplace private and comfortable. Close your eyes and take a few deep breaths. Bring to

mind someone who hurt you and whom you have anger and resentment toward. Now, imagine this person as a child. Ask the young and
innocent version of this person what happened that would cause them
to make the choices they do as an adult. Perhaps ask them, "How were
you hurt, or in what way did you feel abandoned?"

You don't need strength to let go of something.
What you really need is understanding.

-Guy Finley

You can imagine a conversation with the child or perhaps write them a
letter. This exercise allows us to drop our guard and judgments a bit and
let compassion step forward. I'm not saying it will be easy, but if you
stay at it and really do your best with the intention to improve YOUR
life, you'll be amazed at what it will do for you. Turn down the anger,
and turn up the curiosity, compassion, and vibes.

WAY #11

Clean Up and Clear Out

(LAVENDER TO GOLD)

*Tidying your physical space allows
you to tend to your psychological space.*

-Marie Kondo

I wonder if this sounds at all familiar. You wake up in the morning, and before your feet hit the floor, you begin to play out your day in your head. And more than likely, you already feel pressure and stress about whether or not you will get it all done and what could go wrong. You pour a cup of coffee and check your social media feed and/or email (or both) to get your fix. You find, as always, a mix of cute animals, inspiring quotes, and a bunch of shit you REALLY don't care about including selfie posers whom you haven't yet decided to block, and a post or ten that annoy you. Are you with me so far? Most of us are in an agitated state to start off our day. Not only agitated, more to the point, inundated by a swirl of competing thoughts ... AKA, mental clutter.

Now it's time to pick out what you are going to wear. You open your closet, and what do you see? If you're like a lot of us, a jammed-pack and disorganized space. Whether you realize it or not, physical clutter adds to the mental clutter in your brain. The fact is you are in an ongoing, reciprocal relationship with your surroundings. Physical clutter results in mental clutter and vice versa.

Our closets are a microcosm of today's overstuffed world. We are over-scheduled and overthinking. Waaaaaay too much input. As a result, we are in a constant state of prioritizing. We are ruled by the urgent, and sometimes, there truly is no choice. So we push aside the "unimportant" and "trivial" items until "Someday when I have more time." I've got news for you. Over time, the little unfinished projects and cluttered physical spaces accumulate and become big things. They become a major drag on our energy and mood. Good vibe thieves they are.

Clutter, in any form, mental or physical, lowers your vibe. Clearing out raises your frequency.

You can certainly make an effort to filter input and clear out your thinking, and as a fundamental principle, I highly recommend this. But take it from a devout disciple of Overthinkers Anonymous; clearing out the physical clutter is a lot easier. When you clean out and organize your physical space, your thinking becomes more clear and organized. You feel calmed, refreshed, and open.

You use the external form you clean as a template
for your inner psyche. And you elevate a seemingly
mundane chore into a most holy offering.

-Tosha Silver

One of the best and easiest ways to alleviate resistance and pressure in your life and raise your vibe is to clean up and organize something physical that surrounds you. If you want to jump a few levels fast, this will do it. If your closet scares you, start smaller. Clean out and vacuum your car. Choose a drawer and go through it. If you need an item, expect to use it, or if it makes you happy, keep it. If not, put it aside. Ditch what is no longer useful to anyone and drop off the rest to Goodwill. Then, neatly organize what is left.

In *Hello Beautiful*, I share how I periodically take a "little shit day". I take care of a bunch of small, seemingly unimportant tasks because collectively, they do become important. Collectively, they weigh you down and lower your vibe. Unfinished tasks are a form of clutter. When you pause and address them, you lighten your mental and emotional load, and you take that lightness with you in every single thing you do.

Here's a really, really cool bonus to doing this. Not only will you raise your vibe immediately, but you also open up space in your life for more goodness to come in. When you look around and see clutter, you vibrate the feeling of having too much. How is the Universe going to send you the experiences you desire when you have an underlying current of already having too much? My husband and I spent about three hours cleaning out our basement. Within a few weeks, I was presented with an opportunity that netted me five figures. I am sure the two were directly connected. When you remove clutter, you open up room for that which you desire to show up.

> *When they let go of what they didn't need,*
> *what they* did, *could finally arrive.*
>
> -Tosha Silver

Choose something to clean and organize today or choose to take care of multiple "little" unfinished chores. Then, notice and revel in how you feel after you do.

WAY #12

Clean Your Feed

(LAVENDER TO GOLD)

What you feed your mind, will lead your life.

-Kemi Sogunle

We all know that the type and quality of food we eat has a massive influence on how we feel, what we look like, and ultimately our overall health. If we eat a lot of food that is high in fat and cholesterol, we gain weight and clog up our bloodstream. If we consume excessive amounts of sugar, we feel sluggish in the short term, gain weight over the long term, and potentially end up with diabetes. If we eat a lot of food that isn't natural and is loaded with chemicals and preservatives, this too will negatively affect how we feel and look and could lead to health issues. Bottom line, our input directly impacts our output.

We all know this, and I think most of us recognize the need to find the balance (or at least try) that works for us between enjoying the food we love and consuming clean and healthy food. And the better we are at it, the better we look and feel.

Just as important as the type and quality of food we feed our bodies is what we feed our minds. From what we watch on television, what we listen to in the form of radio or podcasts, and what we choose to read, it all influences and affects our mental and emotional states.

It is the food which you furnish to your mind
that determines the whole character of your life.

-Emmet Fox

Front and center for many of us is what our minds consume through social media. (Ironic that it's called our social media "feed.")Most of us would agree we probably spend more time there than we should. It's easy to get sucked in, keep scrolling for the next post, and lose track of time.

Spending time on social media is not necessarily a bad thing. We can stay in touch with others, learn, read or watch heart-warming stories, and definitely laugh. But if we aren't careful, we could end up with a feed that is not balanced. We spend more time reading posts that annoy or aggravate us or make us feel worse about ourselves than posts or videos that inspire us, lift us up, make us happy, feel more confident, and/or allow us to giggle. Our social media feed, if not monitored, can make our thoughts and emotions, in a very real way—unhealthy. It can negatively affect the lens through which we see ourselves, others, and the world.

Every once in a while, it does us good to spend time on social media for the purpose of cleaning up our feed. With awareness and intention, choose to unfollow people and pages that don't enhance your vibe. Even if they're neutral, and you *really don't care* that the person you knew from high school made meatballs last night or their kid or grand-kid graduated from kindergarten, unfollow. It's mental clutter.

In addition to cleaning up your negative vibe feed, take it a step further and search out pages that post positive and inspiring quotes, videos, and stories. This is your trip to the mental organic farm.

The more you feed your mind with positive thoughts,
the more you can attract great things into your life.

-Roy T. Bennett

Clean up your mental feed today. You will instantly raise your vibe today and every day going forward as you consume healthier mind food.

WAY #13

Change Your Tune
(to 528hz)

(BLUE TO GOLD)

*Music can change the world
because it can change people.*

-Bono

It's no secret that the music we listen to greatly affects how we feel. The effect it has on us is sometimes a matter of our personal taste. For example, my husband and I like to listen to streaming music such as Spotify or Pandora. Some of our taste in music is similar. Some isn't. I'm telling you, if we are in the car together and a techno song comes on, he is bopping his head like a happy little camper, and I want to throat punch someone. It grates on me something awful. Sometimes I grin and bear it. It's not all about me. I want him to enjoy what he enjoys. Other times though, I just can't do it. I ask him to skip the song or change the station, which he does. I feel instant relief, and he doesn't get punched. Song changed. Marriage saved.

Other types of music, however, have a universal effect on us. You've no doubt watched scary movies. You just know something is about to go down based on what you hear in the background. Music is deliberately used to amplify the level of fear factor you experience. Then there is music that can pump up just about any person. Listen to Walker Hayes' "Fancy Like" and TRY not to move a muscle. Good luck with that.

It turns out there is another type of music that has a universal effect and has actually been shown to have emotional and physical healing properties. If you think about it, it makes perfect sense. Every cell in our body is affected by frequency and vibration. Sound (music) is vibration at varying frequencies.

The music I am referring to is 528hz, which I accidentally stumbled across after doing yoga to a YouTube video. I had finished my workout, and as I picked up my mat, a video automatically began playing. It showed tropical scenes to 528hz music. Mesmerized, I sat on the floor, staring and listening for a good 10 minutes. Then, I texted a friend whom I knew would appreciate the video. I sent her the link, and she replied, "I always fall asleep to 528." *What? WTF is 528?* I had no idea it was a thing. Thankfully, now I do.

528hz is one of several solfeggio frequencies believed to influence the subconscious and conscious mind, balance energy, and even stimulate healing and emotional release. These frequencies are also believed to release negative energetic blocks. 528hz is known as the frequency of love. It has been shown to give people clarity, increased creativity and immunity, and inner peace. Some practitioners use it for healing and addiction recovery.

> *...since everything is ultimately vibration,*
> *including the human body, then treating vibration*
> *with vibration is logical and elegant.*

> -Eileen Day McKusick

Every single one of us has experienced emotional pain of some sort. It may be something we are consciously aware of or something buried in our subconscious. Either way, it affects how we show up in this world. It's like a bug in the system, a computer virus of sorts. Despite putting in the correct input, something runs amok in the program and prevents us from getting the desired output.

I believe many of our perceived shortcomings, those aspects of ourselves we feel don't measure up and that we'd like to change, aren't something we need to fix or make better. I believe each of us needs self-healing more accurately than self-improvement. When we heal, our lives automatically improve.

So perhaps there is something from your past, maybe even something you think you're over, that still lies below the surface as an energetic block that keeps you from fully experiencing your life as you wish. What if removing that block is like the final click that opens the combination to the treasure that is the true you? And what if all it takes to do so is listening to the right music? Maybe it sounds a little "out there," but what do you have to lose by giving it a shot? It certainly won't hurt, and you may be surprised by how it helps. And honestly, could anything be easier than simply listening to music?

Ah, music, a magic beyond all we do here!

-Albus Dumbledore

Our goal here is to adjust your energetic signal, your vibe. Why not use a tool that itself is composed of energy and vibration? Head to YouTube and search for and listen to some 528hz music. I now play it softly in the background most days as I'm working. Without a doubt, I am in a better-feeling state when I do.

(If this concept intrigues you, check out Eileen McKusick's book, "Tuning the Human Biofield." Prepare, however, to have your mind blown.)

WAY #14

Don't Use Gratitude

(BLUE TO GOLD)

*Appreciation is the purest vibration
that exists on the planet today.*

- Esther Hicks

I'm sure you've heard that in order to (take note of the previous three words) attract more of whatever you desire, practice gratitude for wherever in your life you already have it. For example, if you want more money, practice gratitude for however much you have right now. It is true, and it can work. If you've done this before and not seen the results you hoped for, I believe I know why.

When you attach a strong "in order to" to your gratitude practice, the energy of lack can outweigh the energy of gratitude. When we are far from where we want to be, whether it is how we feel about ourselves or what experiences and people surround us, and we want *so much* for things to be different, we try anything and everything to create change.

But gratitude is both powerful and wise. It knows when it is being used. When you practice gratitude primarily because you hope for a desired outcome, it is like trying to establish a relationship with someone only because you think they can get you closer to something you want. It's fake. There's an ulterior motive at work here, and the gratitude genie knows it.

So while this may seem counterintuitive, I'm suggesting you practice being grateful in the now. Drop your "in order to". It's 100% okay to want more or different. I'm with you there. Ultimately, this book is de-signed to get you closer to all your heart desires. But when you choose to practice gratitude in your life, do your best to let go of the attach-ment to the outcome. Know what you want. Put it out there. Take ac-tion toward your goals. AND, choose to be grateful with the one and only intention of how it feels right now. Let go of the rest. Just. Be. Grateful.

Gratitude is a vibration that resonates with Mother Earth.

-Tracy R. L. O'Flaherty

I've got a few suggestions for how to reap the benefit to your vibe with gratitude:

> -When you catch yourself mindlessly scrolling social media out of boredom, stop. Put your device down. Close your eyes or look around you and come up with three things you are grateful for. You can add even more power to this by writing them down and keeping a running list. I've included space for you to do this at the end of the book. (P 126)

-When you first wake up in the morning and before you climb out of bed, find at least one thing you are grateful for.

-When you lie in bed at night, find something you are grateful for before drifting off to sleep.

-When you wait in line or in traffic, practice gratitude rather than feel rushed or frustrated. You're stuck there anyway. Might as well make good use of the time.

-Put a gratitude jar in a prominent area in your home. Get a glass jar, cut up small pieces of paper and make it a daily practice to write down something you are grateful for, date it, and put it in the jar. Then, on New Year's Eve or Day, sit down and read through them all. It's a phenomenal way to ring in the New Year. You can do this whether you live alone or together with your family. My husband and I each have our own colors, and we have a third color that we invite our guests to use.

Enjoy the little things,
for one day you may look back and realize
they were the big things.

-Robert Brault

Feeling grateful is a terrific Way to kick your vibes into high gear. When you do this consistently and in the most effective manner, both your internal and external conditions will improve. Practicing gratitude is another universal Way, as it effectively raises your vibe no matter your current state.

WAY #15

Be Open to Receive

(BLUE TO GOLD)

Giving is only one-half of the law of increase.
Receiving is the other half.

-Catherine Ponder

When we were little, we were taught that it is better to give than re-ceive. While certainly delivered with good intentions, this childhood lesson we were taught misses the mark a bit.

If we have a program running in the background from a very young age that it's bad to receive, how might that play out? We become adults who over-do, always put others first and ourselves last, and then won-der why we feel exhausted, under-appreciated, and unhappy with ourselves and our lives. If it sounds like I'm talking from first-hand experience, I am.

If the basis of life and the universe is energy, what do you think happens when we don't allow ourselves to receive? We create a short circuit. If all we ever do is focus on giving, we deny ourselves not only the pleasure of receiving, but the natural laws of the universe from functioning as they are meant to.

What might this look like? Struggling to lift something heavy into the back of our car at the home improvement store, and an employee offers to help. "No, thanks. I got it." "Your hair looks great." To which we reply, "I am overdue for a cut," or "Ugh, my hair is so thin." "I love your shoes," garners a "Thanks. I got them on sale." Sound familiar? Think about it, do you almost always reply to a compliment by down-playing it and offers of help by refusing? It's not your fault. It's your conditioning.

These seem like small and insignificant interactions. But in the larger scheme, they aren't so small. You tell the universe, "No, thanks." You create an energetic pattern of rejection.

You want to experience joy and abundance? Practice being open to receive even with the seemingly little things such as a bit of help or a compliment. Allow the natural energy to flow. The next time someone compliments you, smile and say "Thank you." Period. The next time someone offers to help you or be generous, say "Yes." I get that for most of us, it's a whole lot more comfortable to give than receive, but it's essential to allow for the flow of energy in both directions.

If you need another reason to do so, think of this; when you are generous and kind to someone else, doesn't it feel good? Of course, it does. So when you reject help or kindness directed your way, aren't you denying that positive experience to someone else? Yes. You are.

Until we can receive with an open heart,
we are never really giving with an open heart.

-Brené Brown

You are worth happiness and all your heart desires. Validate this to yourself and others. Tell the Universe "Bring it on! I'm open." Let the magic and miracles come your way.

Today, set the intention that you are open to receive, and watch what happens.

WAY #16

Treat Your Body Well

(BLUE TO GOLD)

The groundwork of all happiness is health.

-Leigh Hunt

I bow to and admire you if you are someone who consistently invests in your physical health through exercise and eating right. If, however, you know you could do more to take better care of yourself, you are absolutely, positively not alone.

It's more challenging now than ever due to the stress and anxiety levels many of us experience. Willpower flies right out the window when we are stressed. What we want is relief. We want to soothe ourselves. And that often results in eating comfort food, scrolling social media, binge-watching reality TV while buried under blankets on the couch, or all of the above. There's nothing wrong with any of these ... in moderation. But if this becomes our default mode and results in us putting on extra unwanted pounds, low energy, poor health, and foggy thinking along with the guilt of knowing we are capable of doing better, the very thing that relieves us in the short term also causes us discomfort and pain over the long term.

I'm not here to lecture you on completely changing your habits, nor am I in any position to counsel you on becoming physically healthier. I'm going to guess you already know what you need to do but just haven't yet been able to get yourself to do it. The challenge for many of us is that it seems like a big deal. To think of giving up certain habits and creating all new ones feels daunting. Would I be healthier if I made the radical change to give up all meat and become a vegetarian? Sure. Can I imagine living the rest of my life never again having a Swiss cheeseburger with a side of fries? Nope.

But what if there is another approach, one that doesn't feel so intimidating and difficult? And what if this other approach actually resulted in a much higher success rate over the long term? I believe there is.

What if we looked at getting healthier in tiny increments with small steps and simply kept repeating them? What if we could make just one small choice today that we know is healthier? That feels totally doable, doesn't it? I believe we can, over time, make substantial strides in getting healthier by taking small, believable actions.

If you concentrate on small, manageable steps,
you can cross unimaginable distances.

-Shaun Hick

Part of the challenge for a lot of us is we don't trust ourselves. We don't have a good track record of sticking to our healthy eating or exercise plans. So we lack the confidence of success before we even begin. But what would happen if you let go of the big expectations and started setting small ones? What if, rather than judging yourself based on the outcome, you instead focused on the process? What if today, and just today, you made a healthier choice? You could choose to drink a gallon of water throughout the day, avoid soda or diet soda just for one day, go for a 10- or 15-minute walk, or make a salad for dinner and fill up on that first before your meal. The possibilities are endless.

Big things happen when you do the little things right.

-Don Gabor

The point is, choose something easy and doable, something you KNOW you can do. Don't project forward. Don't worry about what you will or will not do tomorrow. Just today, choose to do something healthier. And at the end of the day, you will reinforce to yourself that you can make healthier choices. Tomorrow when you get up, maybe you will do the same. Now you've got two days in a row to show yourself you are capable. There is real power in this approach as you begin proving to yourself that you can do it by NOT taking on too much. Then, you start seeing results; and before you know it, you've got some momentum.

Think about how great that would feel, and how you feel is exactly what this book is about. So, make a small choice today to do something you know is healthy. Make it easy. Your vibe will rise up the moment you decide what it is and before you even do it. Instant results here.

WAY #17

Be Now-erful

(BLUE TO GOLD)

As soon as you honor the present moment,
all unhappiness and struggle dissolve,
and life begins to flow with joy and ease.

-Eckhart Tolle

There's nothing like the undercurrent of stress and anxiety to tank our vibes. Unfortunately, it also dampens our creativity and productivity and negatively affects us physically. In the short term, this can show up as headaches, a stiff neck or shoulders, and even digestive issues. Over the long term, repeated stress and anxiety can lead to more serious and life-threatening illnesses. Feeling stressed is not a good vibe for enjoying your life and certainly not good for your physical health.

If you want to conquer the anxiety of life,
live in the present moment, live in the breath.

-Amit Ray

You could argue that your stress results from something outside of you. I'm not going to tell you that the people and circumstances around you should never affect how you feel. Of course, they do. The challenge is most of us resign ourselves to the fact that the only way we will ever alleviate our stress (and raise our vibe) is when the people and circumstances around us change. This leaves us feeling powerless, which is very low on the vibrational scale. Stressed and powerless. Who wants to feel like a worked-up victim? Not me.

The issue isn't that you are powerless. It is that you are now-erless.

When we feel stressed, our thoughts are off to the races. They run at lightning speed, in rapid succession, and are usually somewhere else other than the present moment or task at hand. When we are fully present and deliberately focus our thoughts in the moment we are in and on the task or conversation right in front of us, stress and anxiety take a hike. Calm and peace show up. It's simple and certainly powerful but not always so easy.

I will say this a hundred times in a hundred ways (may or may not be exaggerating here), and I hope at least one of those times latches on to you. When you do the inner work to raise your vibration and the thoughts and feelings within you, the people and circumstances around you *will* change. They have to. It is borderline magical. Screw it. It IS magical. YOU are magical. You have an energetic frequency, you are a being of energy, and although that energy is constantly in flux, you have the ability and power to influence it to a higher frequency. When you do, you significantly improve your life experience because you communicate with and affect everything around you on a different level.

So, while I acknowledge you may currently have some less-than-desirable circumstances, if you can open yourself to the possibility that at least some of what I say is true and adopt a few of these practices, your circumstances will change as a result.

You don't always have to figure it out. You don't always have to know how. Make how you feel your number one priority. Do whatever is in your power to feel good NOW and watch what happens. The operative word here is NOW. Your only point of power is this moment. Enter it. Be here.

Worry is a place you go, and it exists only in your mind. When you worry, your thoughts are in the future. Always. Without fail. So, to alleviate some stress and anxiety and adjust your vibration up the scale to feel better NOW and send a frequency to align with more experiences that you enjoy, choose the powerful practice of being present. This means your thoughts join you in this moment, fully aware and focused on whatever you are doing right now.

Doing so requires you to do two things: First, step into the role of the observer of your thoughts.

Rather than being your thoughts and emotions,
be the awareness behind them.

-Eckhart Tolle

Second, when you notice your thoughts are somewhere else, bring them to the present moment. Reel them in. A great way to do this is by engaging your senses. Notice what you hear, feel against your skin, and see. Another easy method is to simply focus on your breath.

When you talk with someone, a co-worker, friend, or family member, be 100% present with them. This *in itself* is an act of kindness. You make that person feel heard and important, and that's a beautiful thing. If you've ever met someone you felt had a high degree of magnetism (ooh, look at THAT word!) I *guarantee* you they were highly present. They made eye contact with you, HEARD what you had to say, really listened rather than having been in their head focused on the next thing they were going to say. Being present with another person is saying, "You matter. I care what you have to say."

You are only here now: you're only alive in this moment.

-Jon Kabat-Zinn

Many people believe if they aren't constantly planning and preparing for the future, nothing will change or get done. You can plan, you can put things in place and work toward something you want to accomplish, *and* you can choose to do that with a high degree of presence of what you are doing right this moment.

Today, as you go about your day, make the conscious decision to keep your awareness and attention in the present. Fully experience the moment you are in, even if it is as simple as taking a shower or sitting at a stop light. I promise you that as you train yourself to do this more and more, your thoughts will slow down, and your stress and anxiety will lessen. And as your stress and anxiety ease, you move up the scale.

There is magic in the now. So, today, show up as your most now-erful self. Take notice of how that feels.

WAY #18

Do Something You Enjoy

(guilt not invited)

(LAVENDER TO GOLD)

*The most important thing is to enjoy your life—
to be happy—it's all that matters.*

-Audrey Hepburn

Do you ever feel guilty about doing what makes you happy? If so, you're not the only one. This is something many of us struggle with, and I have an idea why we do.

Think back to your childhood. Can you remember ever giggling and having a whole lot of fun, and an adult in a much more serious mood came along and yelled at or punished you? Probably a time or hundred. And no blame on the adults here. There are times children might put themselves, others, or property in danger, or a life lesson needs to be taught.

The challenge is before the age of six or seven, our subconscious takes in everything without any filters or judgments. We are walking sponges. So if you were giggling away, having fun, and were yelled at or punished for what you were doing, there's a good chance that imprinted on you, and you formed a belief in response. *Having fun leads to trouble.* We then carry that with us to adulthood, believing if we enjoy ourselves, we just might get in trouble. Makes sense, doesn't it?

On top of that, we live in a time where we largely measure our worth by what we do and accomplish. We believe if we aren't doing, we aren't carrying our weight. We aren't enough. So the cycle continues. We step onto the hamster wheel of accomplishing, expecting that happiness is on a future rung. Spinning, spinning, spinning. Exhausted, stressed, tired, and unhappy. Can you feel me here? So we combine our childhood-born belief that having fun leads to trouble with our current perception of what constitutes our worth, and we've got a nasty witches' brew about guaranteed to keep us from enjoying our lives at all.

Nurturing yourself is not selfish—
it's essential to your survival and your well-being.

-Renée Peterson Trudeau

Do we need to be responsible adults? Of course. And I'm convinced that one of the most responsible things you can do is enjoy your life. Now. Your life is whizzing by. At what point will you pause and realize your joy matters? Your happiness makes you healthier, more loving, creative, and powerful. This is your true nature. It's just hidden under a pile of misconceptions and expectations.

We have come to believe we must sacrifice for those we love and serve them best by working our asses off and providing the financial means to have and do more things. "I want to provide a better life for my children." Maybe "better" needs a new definition.

The fact is, the happier and more joyful you are, the more those around you will be as well. Joy radiates. Laughter is infectious. You want to provide a better life for the people you love? Find ways to enjoy your life more right now. Lead by example. You answer to yourself now. You are the adult in charge of your life.

From simple pleasures like reading a book or taking a bath, to dedicated time to create your art or plant a garden, anything you do that increases your enjoyment of life right now is an investment in yourself, your happiness, *and* the lives of those you love.

Whoever is happy will make others happy too.

-Anne Frank

Today, choose to do something you enjoy without guilt and know it is one of the most intelligent and responsible things you can do.

WAY #19

Release Your Inner Silly

(MAGENTA TO GOLD)

At the height of laughter,
the universe is flung into a kaleidoscope
of new possibilities.

-Jean Houston

Right up there with feeling love and loved as the highest vibration is when we experience something that really makes us laugh. There have been times in my life when I have laughed so hard I had to lean on the person next to me and could barely breathe. Others, where I literally fell to the floor clutching my stomach. As long as I live, I will *never* forget those moments.

If you look back on your life and all the times you really laughed, wouldn't you say that it would make a pretty awesome highlight reel? Think about it. It would literally be a collection of your life experiences with you operating at your highest vibration.

Experiencing moments of laughter are fabulous for raising your vibe and provides all of the benefits of doing so that we discussed in the beginning of this book. But it doesn't end there. Do a simple web search for the benefits of laughter and you will find loads of data on what it does for your mental, emotional, and physical health.

In the short term, you increase oxygen flow to all of your organs, release feel-good endorphins, and alleviate anxiety, pain, and stress. Over the long term, more laughter can improve your immune system, lessen depression, and even boost your self-esteem. Bottom line, you will live a healthier and more enjoyable life and likely a longer one.

So, if it feels amazing to laugh, we treasure these moments and remember them forever, and there is evidence it's actually healthy for us, why not be proactive and look for ways to create more opportunities to laugh?

Laughter is carbonated holiness.

-Anne Lamott

Let me give you some examples of deliberate acts of silliness I've experienced. Maybe something here will inspire you to make yourself and someone else laugh today.

A relative of mine who lives in another state suffered a life-threatening medical condition. Thank God she has since fully recovered. At the time, she was hospitalized for a few weeks and had two young children at home. I flew down to help her husband with their two boys. My husband works full time, and we have a dog, Gingersnap. I needed someone to walk and feed her during the day while I was away and my husband was at work. I made the "mistake" of asking my good friend Amy to help out.

You see, Amy is a major practical joker. This chick is not about things. She is all about experiences and making memorable ones for herself and others. She tells everyone that her favorite day of the year is April 1. What do you think happens when you give the biggest practical joker you know carte blanche access to your home?

My husband, Craig came home one day during the week I was away and immediately noticed the house smelled a bit off. Kind of musty. He greeted Gingersnap, and as he turned the corner into our dining room, strung from one end of the room to the other and back again, were old bras. You read that right. Bras. Probably 30 or 40 of them. My trusted friend went to Goodwill and bought as many used bras as she could and hung them in our dining room. It was freaking hilarious. It was a fantastic comic relief for all of us during a difficult time.

Same girl, different day. We were at my house catching up and having lunch. I failed to notice Amy had an exceptionally large tote bag with her, which, if you know her, is totally out of character. A chap stick in the pocket of her blue jeans is usually about it.

At one point, I stepped outside for a few minutes to walk Ginger. When I came back in, Amy was seated where I left her. All seemed in order. Until after she left. I went to get a coffee cup and found a Barbie in the cabinet. Then later, one shoved in the couch, on the chandelier, you name it. There was even one in the vegetable drawer hanging out with the carrots. Stupid? Yes. Funny? Absolutely.

As fully-grown adults, my husband and I still sometimes hide on each other. Try *not* to laugh when you're hiding and waiting to be discovered.

What is funny about us is precisely that
we take ourselves too seriously.

-Reinhold Neibuhr

There are times when we need to take ourselves and our situations seriously. But I think most of us are so busy adulting and being driven and serious that we forget to have fun along the way. We forget what it was like when we were kids and constantly searching for the next fun thing to do. This life is a journey to be enjoyed. Life doesn't just happen to us. We get to make thousands of choices of what we do and *how* we do our lives. So why not choose to have more fun, lighten up, take ourselves a little or a lot less seriously, and release our inner silly?

The opportunities are endless. Release your inner child, do something silly or play a joke on someone today. You'll pump up your vibes and theirs. You may even create a memory you laugh about for years to come.

WAY #20

Build Your Own Mantra

(LAVENDER TO GOLD)

Be mindful of your self-talk.
It's a conversation with the universe.

- David James

In Way #5, we talked about the power of our words. This is the amped up version.

We know we have an ongoing mental narrative that is often negative. We have discussed the importance of becoming the observer of those thoughts, so we identify with them less and gently move toward the positive.

To change any unwanted behavior, it's not typically enough to simply stop. There needs to be a fill-in, a positive replacement of sorts to fill the void. So while it's absolutely beneficial to observe our negative thoughts and stop them before they build too much momentum, it can further help to develop an inspiring, believable, go-to mantra to reach for any time we catch ourselves should-ing on or doubting ourselves.

Change your self-talk, and you change your life.

-Kristen Helmstetter

A mantra helps remind us about an existing positive aspect of ourselves, including reinforcing our past wins. It speaks to what's possible, what feels good, inspiring, within reach, and believable.

I've created three different mantra builders to guide you on creating one for yourself. You can choose to create one or all three. You can come up with one today that feels right, revisit it in the future, and adjust or build an entirely new one later on. I've created the structure and offered some suggested words to fill in. I've also left room for you to add your own that feel good to you. If you have a favorite word you don't see here, by all means, add it to the list.

The consciousness of "I am" pulsates through
the entire universe. We attract what we are.

-Teresa Mann

Mantra #1

This speaks to your being. What follows your "I am" is one of the most impactful declarations you can make.

Choose one or more verbs below to fill in the blank. A maximum of three allows the phrase to come to mind easily when needed.

"I am_____ (adjective)."

Amazing	Gifted
Beautiful	Grateful
Blessed	Growing
Bold	Improving
Brave	Love
Bright	Loved
Brilliant	A miracle
Capable	Needed
Confident	Not alone
Courageous	Powerful
Creative	Resilient
Determined	Resourceful
A dreamer	Supported
Enough	Successful
Extraordinary	Thoughtful
Fabulous	Unwavering
Fearless	Valuable
Generous	Watched over
Getting better	Whole
A gift	Worthy

_____   _____

_____   _____

_____   _____

Bonus adverbs:

Beautifully	Insanely
Extraordinarily	Incredibly
Fabulously	Perfectly
Gracefully	Remarkably

Mantra #2

"My _____ (choose a word from below)

is_____**."** (choose an adjective from the list of adjectives in Mantra #1)

Confidence   Imagination
Courage   Life
Faith   Mind
Future   Self-worth

A variation on the above is:

"My ability to _____ **is**_____**."**

Mantra #3

"I choose_____**."**

Acceptance   Love
Courage   Me
Faith   Patience
Forgiveness   Peace
Gratitude   Resilience
Kindness

_____   _____

_____   _____

Build one or more today that feel good to you. Then, take it a step further and create a daily alarm on your phone that is (are) the mantra(s) you just built to remind yourself of the goodness you see in yourself, your future, and your life.

WAY #21

Say Yes!

(LAVENDER TO GOLD)

Lean into the little joys when you find them.

-Brianna Wiest

As you come to understand more and more that how you feel is the name of the game, and that feeling good now is the key to feeling good more often and attracting to you more experiences and people that make you happy, you will naturally become more aware of your current feeling state. Your heightened awareness allows you to use this Way to amplify the feelings you enjoy most.

This is one of my favorite Ways to kick my vibes even higher. All I suggest you do is when you recognize a good feeling inside such as love, joy, happiness, peace, relaxation, contentment, say "Yes." That's it. Easy peasy.

Let's explore why this particular vibe-raising method is so effective.

When you actively *look* for your positive experiences and feelings, you raise your awareness to them, and they become the object of your attention and focus. What we focus on expands. You gradually, moment by moment, feeling by feeling, train yourself to recognize when you feel good. As you do, your moments of feeling positive will become more frequent.

Additionally, using the "Yes" practice trains you to bring your awareness to the present moment. This alone raises our vibe, as we've already discussed all the magic and power happens in the present.

It is also a variation of practicing gratitude. You are deliberately paying attention to feeling good, noticing what is happening around you that has aided in this good feeling, and *appreciating* the feelings. What you appreciate, appreciates.

Finally, and most amazingly, you are telling the Universe. "Yes! More of this feeling please!"

When you say yes, the universe helps you.

-Dan Brulé

Here's what this looks like in a typical day in my life:

> -The smell of coffee brewing in the morning. Love this. "Yes."

> -My dog being silly and rolling around on the floor. Warms my heart. "Yes."

-I live in the Northeast. The first day following a cold winter, I step outside, it's almost 50 degrees, and I feel the warmth of the sun on my face. Aaahhh! "Yes."

-A quote I read on Instagram or in a book that causes me to pause and stirs my heart. "Yes."

-The vision for the cover of this book coming to me. I love it, and I know it! "YES!!!"

-A funny text from a friend that makes me laugh. "Yes."

-A quiet evening with no plans, and I pour a glass of wine knowing I can watch whatever show or movie I want or none at all if I so choose. Major aaaahhhh! "Yes."

-Walking out of Home Goods, having bought a few items I loved and only spending $36! Happy! "Yes."

Many of us have been led to believe drastic changes MUST happen to get a taste of happiness. But what if they don't? What if the solution to a seemingly complex issue is actually pretty simple? We are surrounded by moments and opportunities to tune into our higher vibration. We simply need to notice them.

> *A happy life is just a string of happy moments.*
> *But most people don't allow the happy moment,*
> *because they're so busy trying to get a happy life.*
>
> -Abraham-Hicks

I want so much for you to understand that you are never at a loss for choosing what to focus on and how to respond. And I know without a doubt, that as you focus on feeling better and using whatever tools resonate best with you, your life and happiness will come into alignment.

This may happen little by little, but isn't that okay? Isn't knowing this is possible already lifting your vibe? Could you get through the next hour, day, week, knowing you were on the right path? Yes. Yes. Yes. And is it also possible that some significant changes and improvements around you fall into place along the way? Yes.

This may be one of the Ways that becomes a daily practice for you. It is for me.

Day #1

I choose to use Way #_____, which is to

_____.

Notes on what I did, experienced, and noticed:

_____

_____

_____

_____

_____

_____

_____

_____

_____

_____

_____

_____

_____

Day #2

I choose to use Way #_____, which is to

_____.

Notes on what I did, experienced, and noticed:

_____

_____

_____

_____

_____

_____

_____

_____

_____

_____

_____

_____

Day #3

I choose to use Way #_____, which is to

_____.

Notes on what I did, experienced, and noticed:

_____

_____

_____

_____

_____

_____

_____

_____

_____

_____

_____

_____

Day #4

I choose to use Way #_____, which is to

_____.

Notes on what I did, experienced, and noticed:

_____

_____

_____

_____

_____

_____

_____

_____

_____

_____

_____

Day #5

I choose to use Way #_____, which is to

_____.

Notes on what I did, experienced, and noticed:

_____

_____

_____

_____

_____

_____

_____

_____

_____

_____

_____

Day #6

I choose to use Way #_____, which is to

_____.

Notes on what I did, experienced, and noticed:

_____

_____

_____

_____

_____

_____

_____

_____

_____

_____

Day #7

I choose to use Way #_____, which is to

_____.

Notes on what I did, experienced, and noticed:

_____

_____

_____

_____

_____

_____

_____

_____

_____

_____

_____

Day #8

I choose to use Way #_____, which is to

_____.

Notes on what I did, experienced, and noticed:

_____

_____

_____

_____

_____

_____

_____

_____

_____

_____

_____

Day #9

I choose to use Way #_____, which is to

_____.

Notes on what I did, experienced, and noticed:

_____

_____

_____

_____

_____

_____

_____

_____

_____

_____

_____

_____

Day #10

I choose to use Way #_____, which is to

_____.

Notes on what I did, experienced, and noticed:

_____

_____

_____

_____

_____

_____

_____

_____

_____

_____

_____

Day #11

I choose to use Way #_____, which is to

_____.

Notes on what I did, experienced, and noticed:

_____

_____

_____

_____

_____

_____

_____

_____

_____

_____

_____

Day #12

I choose to use Way #_____, which is to

_____.

Notes on what I did, experienced, and noticed:

_____

_____

_____

_____

_____

_____

_____

_____

_____

_____

_____

Day #13

I choose to use Way #_____, which is to

_____.

Notes on what I did, experienced, and noticed:

_____

_____

_____

_____

_____

_____

_____

_____

_____

_____

_____

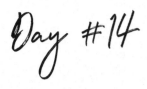

Day #14

I choose to use Way #_____, which is to
_____.

Notes on what I did, experienced, and noticed:

_____

_____

_____

_____

_____

_____

_____

_____

_____

_____

_____

_____

_____

Day #15

I choose to use Way #_____, which is to

_____.

Notes on what I did, experienced, and noticed:

_____

_____

_____

_____

_____

_____

_____

_____

_____

_____

_____

Day #16

I choose to use Way #_____, which is to

_____.

Notes on what I did, experienced, and noticed:

_____

_____

_____

_____

_____

_____

_____

_____

_____

_____

_____

_____

Day #17

I choose to use Way #_____, which is to

_____.

Notes on what I did, experienced, and noticed:

_____

_____

_____

_____

_____

_____

_____

_____

_____

_____

_____

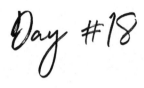

Day #18

I choose to use Way #_____, which is to

_____.

Notes on what I did, experienced, and noticed:

_____

_____

_____

_____

_____

_____

_____

_____

_____

_____

_____

_____

Day #19

I choose to use Way #_____, which is to

_____.

Notes on what I did, experienced, and noticed:

_____

_____

_____

_____

_____

_____

_____

_____

_____

_____

_____

Day #20

I choose to use Way #_____, which is to
_____.

Notes on what I did, experienced, and noticed:

_____

_____

_____

_____

_____

_____

_____

_____

_____

_____

_____

Day #21

I choose to use Way #_____, which is to

_____.

Notes on what I did, experienced, and noticed:

_____

_____

_____

_____

_____

_____

_____

_____

_____

_____

_____

I am grateful for:

_____   _____

_____   _____

_____   _____

_____   _____

_____   _____

_____   _____

_____   _____

_____   _____

_____   _____

_____   _____

_____   _____

_____   _____

About the Author

Keryl Pesce is the founder of Little Pink Press, a publishing company which supports books written by or for women. She is the co-host of the award-winning talk show, *Happy Hour*, which airs on K104.7FM in the Hudson Valley. She love the color pink, blue jeans and graphic tees, and Swiss cheese burgers.

Other books by Keryl:

Happy Bitch
Hello Beautiful
Pink Pretty Thoughts
Happiness Journal
Share this Journal (co-authored with Amy Gopel)

www.kerylpesce.com

Come hang out with me!

Join me on Instagram, @kerylpesce, and I'll continue to share ideas, tips, quotes, and insights to support you in your journey.

Made in the USA
Coppell, TX
02 August 2022

80792850R00075